CLB 2333
© 1989 Colour Library Books Ltd, Godalming, Surrey
© 1989 Illustrations: Oxford Scientific Films Ltd, Long Hanborough, Oxford
Colour separation by Hong Kong Graphic Arts Ltd, Hong Kong
Printed and bound in Italy by Fratelli Spada SpA
All rights reserved
ISBN 0 86283 692 1

· Oxford Scientific Films ·

ANTARCTIC WILDLIFE

Ben Osborne

· *Colour Library Books* ·

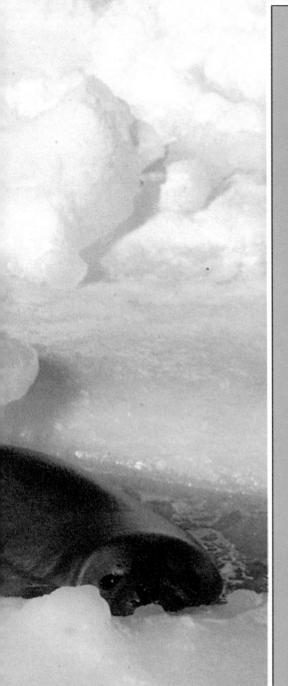

Contents

Previous page: wandering albatross chicks are raised through the winter on sub-Antarctic islands, in this case South Georgia.

These pages: a Weddell seal with her month-old pup.

1

The Frozen Continent

Antarctica is the coldest continent on earth. It consists of a huge *icecap* which surrounds the South Pole. The ice rests on a continental landmass and may reach a thickness of three kilometres. Occasionally, rocky peaks project through the ice to provide a solid surface on which lichens may grow. Elsewhere, the ice cap is a frozen, lifeless desert.

The weight of ice in the middle of Antarctica pushes the coastal ice outwards, towards the sea. Enormous glaciers, often several kilometres across, flow steadily downwards from the central plateau, cracking and collapsing as they pass over rocky ridges deep under the ice. Where the glaciers meet the sea the ice floats, forming large ice shelves which often extend a considerable distance out to sea. Eventually, the continual pressure of ice from the glaciers forces the ice shelf to split into chunks which break away to form icebergs. These can be

anything from a small 'growler' a metre across, up to a huge 'tabular' berg with an area of several hundred square kilometres.

Although most of the coastline of Antarctica is a continuous ice shelf, there are areas where the ice cover is not so great. Along the Antarctic Peninsula – the finger of land that branches off the main continent – the glaciers are separated by fierce mountains. At sea level, promontories of exposed rock extend outwards from the foot of the mountains, creating an area free of ice on which penguins can breed and seals can haul out of the water to bask in the sun.

Beyond the coast lies the Antarctic Ocean. These waters have a reputation among sailors for being some of the most dangerous in the world. Yet to most of the creatures that inhabit this inhospitable region, the sea is the source of life. Under the stormy waters of the Antarctic Ocean there is a highly productive biological system, based upon a small, shrimp-like animal called krill, which supports not only the larger marine animals like whales and seals, but most of the seabirds as well.

Icebergs drift away from the coast, gradually melting to form strange shapes.

Above: a mosaic of evening light, as the fast ice breaks up to form ice floes.

Left: an iceberg lies trapped in the sea ice during the Antarctic winter.

A number of small, isolated islands break the monotony of the Antarctic Ocean. The largest of these is South Georgia, which is situated 960 kilometres east of the Falkland Islands. South Georgia, like the other windswept sub-Antarctic islands, is a tremendously important breeding site for many of the seabirds and seals that feed in the southern oceans but need to come ashore to breed.

2
Survival Down South

Antarctica suffers the worst weather in the world. The main problem is the cold. Temperatures around the coast remain at or below freezing point in summer and drop to an average of -20°C in winter. Inland, the conditions are even more severe, with temperatures as low as -80°C being recorded at the South Pole. These extremes of temperature are exaggerated by frequent storms during which the chilling effect of the wind can reduce the apparent temperature to well below -100°C. Also, being a polar region, the long summer days, when the sun never sets, are balanced by months of darkness through the freezing winter.

To cope with these extremes, the animals which live in Antarctica have evolved special *adaptations* to conserve body heat. Penguins, for example, have short, stubby feathers which provide a wind-resistant outer surface. At the base of their feathers there is a tuft of soft down which traps a layer of warm air next to the skin and prevents heat escaping. Emperor penguins, which have to withstand colder conditions than other penguins, have twelve feathers per square centimetre ensuring eighty-four per cent of their *insulation*. The rest is gained from the substantial layer of *blubber* just under their skin. This is an

Conditions in the Antarctic can be very severe, especially when the wind blows loose snow across the ice.

advantage that penguins have over other birds. Being flightless, their weight is not critical, so they can easily carry more blubber than other seabirds.

Only in the chick stages do flying seabirds accumulate a blubber layer. A spectacular example of this is the wandering albatross chick, which is raised through the long Antarctic winter. These chicks have a wonderfully thick down coat which provides much of their insulation. However, they also store plenty of fat, which enhances their ability to retain heat and enables them to survive long periods of fasting when the parents are away at sea.

Seals depend heavily on blubber to insulate them while they are at sea and when they haul out on ice floes. They also have a layer of fur which protects them from the wind. But what happens when the wind calms down and the sun shines? It doesn't happen often, but when the weather conditions are comparatively mild, many Antarctic animals suffer from heat stress.

Below: blubber provides important insulation for this Weddell seal.

Bottom: emperor penguins huddle together to conserve heat during the Antarctic winter.

The obvious answer is to jump into the sea to cool off. But there are certain times of year when they must stay ashore. Seals may have to guard new-born pups and penguins cannot leave the nest while they are incubating, so they have developed mechanisms to prevent over-heating.

Elephant seals suffer particularly badly from heat stress as they live in a milder environment than other Antarctic seals and have a very thick layer of blubber. When it gets hot, they flick sand or gravel onto their backs. This shades them from the direct rays of the sun and prevents them from over-heating.

Penguins lose heat by *dilating* the blood vessels near the skin. This increases the blood supply to the surface of the penguin's body, where the cold air cools the blood and thus reduces the body temperature. Heat loss may be maximised by holding the flippers away from the body, which allows cold air to circulate around a greater area of skin surface.

ANTARCTIC WILDLIFE

3

Life in the Sea

Looking at its cold, grey surface, it is hard to imagine the fantastic variety of life that exists in the Antarctic Ocean. Thick green clouds of phytoplankton, strange, orange sea spiders, shimmering translucent ctenophores, colourless ice fish, seals, whales and many other creatures all thrive in the waters around Antarctica.

The Antarctic Ocean is very fertile. Cold water carries high concentrations of oxygen which, together with the long hours of daylight in summer, provides an ideal environment for plant growth. Free-floating phytoplankton proliferates rapidly in these conditions and forms dense 'blooms' – a kind of thick soup of plant material. A number of small marine animals feed on *phytoplankton*, the most important being a shrimp called krill. This one animal is the key to the Antarctic food chain, as it is eaten by practically all higher animals in the Antarctic.

Krill are about four centimetres long and semi-transparent. They spawn from January to March. The eggs are released near the water surface, after which they sink into deep water, developing as they go. Deep-water currents convey the developing eggs to the edge of the continental landmass where they hatch. The young pass through two larval stages before re-appearing at the surface of the ocean as juvenile krill.

Being at the mercy of ocean currents, krill tend to be concentrated into huge swarms, which may cover an area of several square kilometres and incorporate millions of tonnes of krill. Not surprisingly, these swarms attract the attention of whales, seals, albatrosses, penguins and petrels, as well as the krill's closer neighbours, fish and squid, all of which rely on krill as a major source of food.

Deep down on the sea bed, far below the comparatively frantic activity near the surface, life is very different. Molluscs glide slowly over the rocks, grazing on the thick, green algae which gathers nutrients from the surrounding water. A colourful mosaic of corals and sponges encrust exposed rock ledges, while delicate orange sea anemones stun their tiny prey animals as they drift past. Long-legged sea spiders and heavily-armoured isopods pick their way carefully through this colourful scene, alert for stray items of food.

In shallower waters near offshore islands this prolific seabed fauna is constantly threatened with destruction. Large icebergs may be dragged along the ocean floor as they enter shallow water and can devastate huge areas of the seabed, which may take many years to recover. To avoid the damaging effects of icebergs, many *benthic* animals descend to deeper offshore waters in winter.

Above: an anemone clings to a rock in shallow water close inshore.

Facing page top: some of the most colourful wildlife in the Antarctic is found on the sea bed.

Facing page bottom: the ice fish lacks haemoglobin in its blood, resulting in a colourless appearance in its gills and internal organs.

4
The Largest Animals on Earth.

During the southern summer the Antarctic Ocean is the home of the great whales. The largest of these is the blue whale, now very rare, which measures up to thirty metres in length and can weigh up to 180 tonnes. Much more common is the smaller humpback whale, which is just over half the size of the blue whale. Humpbacks breed in temperate and tropical regions, but migrate to Antarctic waters in summer when krill is plentiful.

It seems strange that such a huge animal should live off a tiny shrimp, yet these whales have evolved a special feeding mechanism which allows them to scoop up enormous quantities of krill from the sea. In the whale's mouth there is a series of filters called baleen plates. The whale takes in huge mouthfuls of water, and sieves out the shrimps by bringing its tongue up against the roof of its mouth. This expels the water, leaving the shrimps caught in the baleen plates. Because krill occur in dense shoals, whales can feed very efficiently using this method.

Above: steam rises from the back of a sleeping humpback whale. The picture was taken just after the whale had breathed out through its twin nostrils.

Left: a humpback whale blows as it swims past a glacier snout.

*Two humpback whales rest with their
knobbly heads out of the water*

Although baleen whales feed mostly on krill, they can also take fish. This requires a slightly more sophisticated feeding mechanism. One method, unique to humpback whales, is to blow a ring of bubbles around a shoal of fish. The fish react to the bubbles by clustering together within the ring, thus concentrating themselves into a convenient mouthful for the whale.

Whales with baleen plates are called baleen whales. The other major group of whales is called the toothed whales. This includes the sperm whales, killer whales and most of the dolphins. Unlike the baleen whales, these species feed on animals higher up the food chain than krill. Sperm whales favour large squid, while killers cruise the edge of the ice shelf looking for penguins and young seals.

Following a century of exploitation by man, whales are much less common than they used to be. The whales that were most easily harpooned or those that yielded the most oil are the rarest. Thus the slow-moving and conspicuous southern right whale and humpback whale are at seriously low population levels. Current estimates put the blue whale population at around 1,000 individuals, compared with a figure of about 200,000 at the end of the last century.

5
On the Edge of the Ice

In winter, the seas around Antarctica freeze over. The sea ice can reach a depth of several metres, but it breaks up during the summer to form ice floes. Some species of seal are associated with this area of *pack ice*.

Crabeater seals are one of the most numerous large mammals in the Antarctic, with an estimated population of 40 million. They gather along the edge of the ice, often hauling out in large groups on the floes. Although their name suggests it, they do not eat crabs, concentrating instead on krill and, to a lesser extent, fish. Their teeth are serrated, which allows them to strain the krill from the water in much the same way as whales use their baleen plates.

The crabeater is a true Antarctic species, using the ice floes as its breeding ground. In the spring the females will haul out onto a floe to pup. Meanwhile, a male will defend the *floe* and an underwater territory around it. During four weeks of suckling the pup grows rapidly from twenty to 113 kilograms. After the pup is *weaned*,

The crabeater seal is the most numerous seal in the Antarctic.

it takes to the water and has to adapt quickly to its new environment as there are some fearsome predators lurking along the ice margins, of which killer whales are the most dangerous. Indeed, there are few adult crabeaters that do not bear the scars of an early encounter with a killer whale.

The Weddell seal is another species that favours the ice-bound waters close to the Antarctic continent. During the winter Weddell seals will keep a breathing hole open in the sea ice. As the hole freezes the seal will gnaw away the ice until it has re-opened the space and can, if necessary, haul out of the sea onto the ice. This is particularly important in the early spring, when the seals give birth to their pups. Weddell seals are very good divers, reaching depths of up to 600 metres. In the cold, dark depths they find the fish and squid that form the bulk of their diet.

Above: lying on the ice, a young Weddell seal pup shelters beside its mother.

Right: crabeater seals swim below the sea ice.

Two other seals occur along the ice edge, though little is known about either of them. The leopard seal is sleek and fast and has a reputation as a voracious *predator*, taking anything that comes its way, including young crabeater seals. The Ross seal is very rarely seen, partly because it lives in the thickest areas of pack ice.

ANTARCTIC WILDLIFE

6

Beachmasters

A large bull elephant seal keeps a watchful eye on his densely-packed harem, ready to fend off any male intruders.

The beaches of the sub-Antarctic islands provide a dirty, muddy, noisy and smelly contrast to the clean, white purity of the pack ice. These beaches are the favoured breeding grounds of the southern elephant seal and the Antarctic fur seal.

The coastline of South Georgia is quiet in the winter. A huddle of gentoo penguins might occupy one corner of a beach. A group of blue-eyed shags could be seen perched on a rocky headland. But there is nothing overpowering about it – except the views.

By early October, however, the elephant seals have started to arrive, and the beaches at once become a scene of conflict as males fight for positions on the main breeding beaches. When the females come ashore the larger males fight bloody battles, the reward being to maintain a territory on the part of the beach where the females are pupping. Dominant males, called beachmasters, will mate with the females after they have pupped.

At the height of the breeding season a popular beach will be literally covered with a solid mass of seals. However, each beachmaster will recognise his own *harem* and will know where the dividing line lies between his own females and those of the neighbouring male – even though, to the casual observer, it is a continuous mass of animals.

After they have bred and the *pups* are weaned, elephant seals go to sea to feed. Both males and females will be weakened by the effort of fighting or raising pups and will need to gain weight before hauling out in the autumn to moult. When moulting, they lie in placid heaps, called 'pods', which are very different from the noisy, aggressive harems that formed during the breeding season.

Compared to adult elephant seals, which can weigh four tonnes and reach a length of five metres, Antarctic fur seals are diminuitive creatures. However, what they lack in size they make up for in mobility and aggression. While other seals are slow and cumbersome on land and can be avoided by walking away if chased, it is a different matter with fur seals. Indeed, you would need to run fairly fast to avoid being caught by a charging bull.

A 'beachmaster' fur seal bull defends his patch of beach at the start of the breeding season.

A young male fur seal takes refuge on the tussocky slopes of South Georgia, away from the aggressive scenes on the breeding beaches below

The fur seal breeding season starts in November, when elephant seals have returned to the sea. Like the elephant seal, males come ashore before the females and fight to hold a territory on one of the beaches where they know the females will pup. Soon after the first few females have hauled out, every square metre of beach will be defended by a male.

Soon after her pup is born the female will go to sea to feed. These feeding trips typically last for only a few days, but if food is in short supply the female will take much longer to replenish the food reserves she needs in order to *suckle* her pup. If, however, she is absent for too long her pup may starve, providing a meal for one of the many scavengers that inhabit the beaches alongside the seals.

Elephant seal bulls fight bloody battles at the onset of the breeding season. The winner establishes a territory on the beach and will mate with the cows when they haul out.

7
Penguins – Underwater Fliers

Penguins are among the most characteristic and abundant birds of the Antarctic. With their comical appearance they have earned a popular reputation as gentle and lovable subjects of cartoons and greeting cards. In the wild this endearing image is quickly dispelled.

Penguins are most easily seen on their breeding grounds. They gather in huge colonies, called rookeries, where they argue noisily over nest sites, fiercely evicting passers-by that enter their territory, and *regurgitate* half-digested meals of krill to feed their chicks. They also smell, the result of an enormous build-up of guano around the rookery. Indeed, visitors usually smell penguin rookeries well before they come within sight of them.

Penguins have adapted superbly to the rigorous Antarctic environment in a number of ways. They have developed a very sophisticated insulation system to combat the cold, their paddle-like flippers are ideal for underwater propulsion and they are able to dive to great depths. In accomplishing these changes, they have sacrificed the ability to fly, but their superlative underwater performance gives them greater prey-gathering opportunities and, usually, enough speed to avoid predation.

The four smaller Antarctic penguins – gentoo, Adélie, chinstrap and macaroni – all breed during the summer, coming ashore in spring to start courtship and nest-building. The rookeries are usually situated on exposed promontories where the wind prevents an excessive build-up of snow, thus ensuring that the rock is uncovered when they start to occupy the nest sites. Nests consist of a low mound of pebbles in which there is a shallow, bowl-shaped scoop, thinly lined with softer materials such as tail feathers and moss. Penguins will often dispute the ownership of nest material, and neighbouring birds will frequently steal pebbles from each other's nests.

These species generally lay two eggs, though in the case of macaroni penguins the first-laid egg normally fails to hatch, leaving the larger,

A gentoo penguin with her three-week-old chicks.

second-laid egg to produce the single chick. Gentoos, on the other hand, produce two eggs of similar size and will raise two chicks in a good season. In a poor season, for example when krill is less plentiful, one or both chicks may die if the parents cannot find enough food to support them.

Although they are of comparable size and breed in similar areas, gentoo and macaroni penguins feed in very different ways. Gentoos feed in the shallow waters within thirty kilometres of the coast while macaronis go further afield, finding prey in deeper water up to a hundred kilometres offshore. Gentoos are rarely away feeding for more than ten hours. Macaroni penguins, however, stay away for up to forty hours.

Each strategy has its advantages and disadvantages. Gentoos do not spend so much time travelling, but they do not range far enough to be certain of finding krill. The greater range of the macaroni penguins ensures that they will find krill, though they may expend more effort

Looking like a miniature torpedo, a gentoo penguin is superbly designed for swimming under water.

finding it. This gives the macaronis a more certain food supply but one which costs more to obtain. The advantage is that they are less affected by the exact position of krill swarms. The disadvantage is that they can only obtain enough food to raise one chick. The gentoos, on the other hand, by expending less effort on feeding, suffer badly when the krill swarms do not come close enough to their rookeries. In such a year gentoos may not even manage to raise a single chick. However, in a good year they can raise two chicks.

The rookeries are empty during the winter, though gentoos will usually remain nearby, especially around the sub-Antarctic islands. The other species will be out at sea, around the edge of the pack ice or further north, putting on weight in preparation for the next breeding season.

A group of Adélie penguins leaps ashore onto the icy shores of Antarctica.

8

Emperor Penguins

In the frozen twilight of the Antarctic night emperor penguins huddle close together. They bow their heads to avoid the piercing cold that grips the ice on which they patiently *incubate* their eggs. The searching spotlight of the torch beam shows areas of green snow. These are patches of guano which represent the remains of the Emperors' last meal two months ago, a briefly-snatched morsel of squid taken in the cold, dark waters 200 metres below the stormy surface of the Antarctic Ocean.

Emperor penguins are the giants of the penguin world. They stand 1.2 metres high and weigh up to forty-five kilograms. Unlike other penguins, emperors breed on winter *fast-ice*, below the huge ice cliffs that mark the edge of the Antarctic ice shelf. They breed in winter, when the ice is most stable, and endure an average temperature of minus 20°C, which is colder than the temperature inside a domestic deep freeze. Strong winds and frequent blizzards add to the harshness of the weather.

After the female has laid the single egg she returns to the sea, leaving the male to do the incubation. To keep the egg warm, the male lifts it onto his feet and tucks it into a brood pouch between his legs. This has two advantages – emperor penguins don't need to build nests, and they can move around while incubating.

Although the emperor is very well insulated, with a thick layer of *downy* feathers next to the skin, it is still important for it to conserve heat by any means possible. So the incubating males crowd together in compact huddles, thereby reducing their individual heat loss. This kind of social behaviour is very unusual and is unique among penguins, which are usually very aggressive towards each other.

While incubating, the males cannot feed, so that by the time the chick is ready to hatch the male will have starved for just over two months – an incredible feat of endurance given the savage environmental conditions. By now the females have returned, and they take over the

parental responsibilities while the males go to sea for a month to replace their exhausted fat reserves. Both parents then take turns, with one guarding the chick and the other feeding at sea. At six weeks the chick is old enough to fend for itself and will join other chicks as they gather in *creches*, a behaviour pattern found in most species of penguin.

By mid-summer the chicks have lost their down and, although they are only half the adult weight, they are ready to go to sea. Here lies the advantage of breeding in winter: mid-summer is the time when food is most plentiful, so it is a good time for the chicks to become independent. If emperors bred during summer the chicks would go to sea in mid-winter when food is hard to find. As it is, only four out of ten emperor chicks survive to maturity, the others succumbing to starvation, cold, disease and predation.

Above: an emperor penguin feeds its four-month-old chick.

Facing page top: emperor penguins incubate their eggs on their feet, below the ice cliffs at the edge of the Antarctic continent.

Facing page bottom: when their parents are feeding at sea, emperor penguin chicks gather in creches, huddling together to avoid the chilling effects of the wind.

9

Albatrosses

In his poem *The Ancient Mariner* Coleridge describes how the shooting of an albatross leads to a series of dreadful disasters on board a sailing ship. The species he had in mind was probably the sooty albatross, which belongs to a group known as the mollymawks. These are the smaller albatrosses, three species of which occur throughout the southern oceans and breed on sub-Antarctic islands.

Albatrosses depend entirely on the sea for food, flying incredible distances in their search for krill, fish, squid and lamprey. As the distances they cover are enormous, they are perfectly adapted to flying over the sea. By clever use of the wind and waves they can fly both fast and efficiently.

Albatross flight is called 'dynamic soaring'. It starts with a descent, during which the bird gathers speed. When it is just above the water surface the bird levels out to a horizontal flight along the line of the wave. As the wave moves forward it creates a cushion of air in front of it. The albatross is able to maintain a position just above the wave and is partly supported by the air cushion. However, the bird will gradually lose speed during this horizontal flight so will finally turn into the wind to gain height before making another downward flight to gain speed once again.

This dependence on both wind and waves is probably why albatrosses are confined to the southern oceans – they have never been able to fly through the calm equatorial waters to reach the northern hemisphere.

Although their home is the middle of the ocean, albatrosses must come ashore to breed. Not surprisingly, they come to the windswept islands of the sub-Antarctic, as these are near to their food source and there is plenty of wind to enable them to take off.

The more common Antarctic mollymawks, the grey-headed and black-browed albatrosses, breed in compact colonies. Their nests are made of peaty earth and are built on a little pedestal to help drain the nest when it rains. They lay only one egg, which is laid in the spring, and the chick is raised during the summer. At first one parent stays with the chick to protect it from marauding predators such as giant petrels and brown skuas, but as it becomes more capable of defending itself both parents will head out to sea, returning every few days to feed the chick. By the autumn the chicks are fully grown and have replaced their down with a set of flight feathers. One day the parents will no longer return with food and the chick is left to fly off on its own, leaving the colony deserted until the following spring.

Above: light-mantled sooty albatrosses nest on sub-Antarctic islands. This well-grown chick waits for its parents to bring back a meal.

Facing page top: light-mantled sooty albatrosses are among the more agile aerial performers.

Facing page bottom: adult black-browed albatrosses guard young chicks in a colony on Bird Island, South Georgia.

10
Ocean Wanderers

Wandering albatrosses are true ocean travellers who spend most of their lives at sea. They are most frequently seen gliding along behind ships, on the lookout for scraps. Weighing in at around ten kilograms and with a wingspan of up to three metres, the wandering albatross is one of the largest birds on earth.

Like the smaller mollymawks, wanderers breed on sub-Antarctic islands, but because of their tremendous size their breeding cycle is very different. The problem is that the chicks cannot grow quickly enough to reach full size within the short summer season. So they start their breeding season much later than the mollymawks, and the chicks are hatched in the autumn. The adults feed the chicks right through the winter and they *fledge* the following spring, 275 days after hatching.

When the chicks leave the island they are on their own. In the last few weeks at the nest they will have practised using their wings and may have made a few short flights. But the final launch from a cliff top into a completely alien world is a dramatic one and they often spend some time testing the wind before they take the plunge. They adapt quickly, however, and will spend the first three years of their life at sea, landing only to feed or when they are becalmed.

Wanderers are remarkable navigators. As they reach maturity they will find their way back to the island where they hatched as chicks three years previously. For a further three or four years the young albatross will return to the island in the summer to search for a mate. The courtship process is lengthy, but wanderers pair for life so it is important to find the right partner. Wanderers finally start to breed at the age of seven, or a little later.

Young wandering albatrosses display near a nest site on South Georgia.

Above: a male wandering albatross sky-calls as part of its courtship display.

Top: although clumsy on land, wandering albatrosses are magnificent fliers, spending most of their time at sea in the southern oceans.

After spending the spring building a nest, the egg is laid in mid-summer. A three-month incubation period follows, with both adults taking turns to sit on the egg while their partner is at sea. The chick hatches in March, the Antarctic autumn, and is guarded by one of the parents until it is large enough to fend off predators.

It is then left on its own, except for when one of its parents returns from the sea with a meal.

If it hasn't been fed for a while the chick goes frantic when the adult arrives, making desperate, squeaking noises and tapping the parent's bill to encourage it to regurgitate some food. Despite the physical awkwardness of passing half-digested squid and fish by interlocking bills, there is rarely any spillage.

It is remarkable what wanderers manage to find in their travels, and many items that turn up in food samples (e.g. cabbage stalks, leeks, chocolate wrappers) can only have been scavenged from rubbish dumped overboard by ships.

11
A Wealth of Seabirds

Penguins and albatrosses might be the most unusual seabirds of the Antarctic region, but they are by no means the only ones. A wide range of seabirds has adapted to the rigorous *environmental* conditions and the apparent lack of nest sites.

The Antarctic petrel and the snow petrel are both birds of the ice, feeding on krill in the southernmost areas of open water along the edge of the pack ice. Both nest on the Antarctic continent, often far inland; wherever there is an isolated rock spire sticking out of the ice they will find a crevice in which to create a rudimentary nest.

Antarctic terns flit between chunks of ice along the shoreline, dipping into the shallow water for small crustaceans and other prey.

Top: a snow petrel flies through the clear blue skies above Antarctica.

Above: a blue-eyed shag carries nest material to the colony during the early stages of the breeding season.

calories needed to keep the little bird warm. Of course, like all other Antarctic birds, it is also well insulated by a layer of soft, downy feathers next to the skin.

The sub-Antarctic islands are an oasis for many Antarctic petrels, especially those that nest in burrows. The Antarctic continent has no significant soil in which these birds can dig their nest-hole, but the tussocky grassland on South Georgia and other islands is ideal.

Most of the burrowing birds, for example white-chinned petrels, blue petrels and dove prions, feed during the day and only come ashore at night, when they can escape the attention of predators. It is therefore difficult to estimate their numbers (unlike penguins and albatrosses, which can be counted easily as they sit on their nests). However, if you go up into the tussock grassland at night you can hear the returning birds greet their mates in the burrows. The sound is deafening as the hillsides are riddled with burrows. No-one knows exactly how the birds find their way back to the burrows in the darkness, but it is possible that they arrive near the island at dusk and then locate their burrows by smell. This would explain why many more come ashore on misty nights, when scents are exaggerated, than on dry nights.

Sometimes large flocks of dove prions gather near the coast, feeding where water currents carry tiny creatures to the surface. These flocks can number tens of thousands of birds, giving the impression of a swarm of locusts.

Southern black-backed gulls, Antarctic terns and blue-eyed shags also frequent the coastal waters. Shags nest in compact colonies, often closely associated with penguin rookeries. They feed inshore, taking fish from the dense beds of kelp that choke the shallower water. Antarctic terns dip and dive gracefully between the broken chunks of ice along the tideline, picking up small crustaceans from the disturbed water, while the ubiquitous gulls take whatever is going, some feeding at sea, others jostling among the other scavengers as they search the beaches for carrion.

The diminutive Wilson's storm petrel is often seen dancing along the surface of the water, picking up droplets of oil or tiny marine micro-organisms. At only a few ounces it is the smallest of the Antarctic seabirds, with a wingspan about twice the length of a wandering albatross's bill. Small animals do not usually do well in cold conditions, having a large surface area per unit bodyweight (which means that they lose heat more quickly than a larger animal), but the Wilson's storm petrel manages to survive by obtaining a high-energy diet. This provides the

12
Antarctic Pirates

Life is tough in the Antarctic. Many animals die from lack of food and the cold, as well as the stress of fighting and, of course, old age. This provides a bonanza for the scavengers, most of which breed near an obvious potential food source, like a penguin rookery or a seal colony.

Most of the scavengers are large and aggressive and will hover round a dying animal waiting until it is so weak that it cannot defend itself. Then they start to pull it apart. The experts are the giant petrels, huge ugly brutes with a mean glint in their beady eyes. They will peck at areas of thin skin until they can force their head into the carcase. Then they pull out all the intestines and meat, leaving just bones and skin. The dominant birds push their way in first, and only when they are full will they let their subordinates feed.

As an Adélie penguin feeds its chick, a sheathbill flies in and intercepts the food.

A floating elephant seal carcase attracts a large crowd of scavengers, mainly giant petrels and Cape pigeons.

Amidst the squabbling giant petrels the predatory brown skuas hover, always on the lookout for a spare morsel of meat. They cannot compete with the much larger giant petrels, however, and usually look elsewhere for a meal – for penguin eggs and chicks, burrowing petrels, albatross eggs, and even other skua chicks.

Skuas are great opportunists, taking practically anything. Individual birds may develop very specific feeding techniques which require practice but can be very rewarding. Some capitalise on the defence reaction of albatross chicks – which is to vomit a nasty, oily mixture onto an attacker. The skuas will taunt the albatross chick until it regurgitates, stepping aside smartly so that they don't get covered in oil, and then, when the chick has emptied its stomach, will pick this good, hot meal off the ground.

The small, white sheathbill has a similar trick. These birds wait until an adult penguin is feeding its chick and will intercept the food as it is passed from parent to chick by flying in at the crucial moment when the food is being passed.

Both skuas and gulls take advantage of man's presence in the Antarctic as they gather round any base, waiting for scraps from the kitchen. They become quite cheeky and will even take food from the hand. Indeed, the *territory* immediately outside the kitchen window of the British Antarctic Survey base became one of the most sought after skua territories on South Georgia.

13
Wildlife in Danger.

Ever since its discovery in 1820, Antarctica has suffered at the hands of man. The early visitors were interested primarily in whales for their oil and meat, and seals for their furs. In those days there were plenty of animals and relatively few ships. Soon, however, as more and more companies began to operate in the southern oceans, pressure on whales and seals became intense and eventually resulted in their virtual extermination. Sealing finally stopped at the end of the last century, but the Japanese whaling fleet has continued to take whales from Antarctic waters until recently.

During this period of intense exploitation, a number of shore stations were established, both on the Antarctic continent and on many of the sub-Antarctic islands. Once thriving communities, these stations are now derelict ghost towns inhabited only by mice and rats. On South Georgia, where the Norwegians established a number of whaling stations, reindeer were introduced as a source of meat.

Reindeer were introduced to South Georgia as a source of meat. They have since destroyed large areas of coastal grassland which used to hold important colonies of burrowing seabirds.

Above: a fur seal suffers terrible injuries when a piece of net becomes caught over its head

Facing page top: the abandoned whaling station at Leith Harbour used to be the focus of whaling activities in the South Atlantic.

Facing page bottom: the legacy of Antarctic whaling – bleached whale vertebrae lie on a beach at Cuverville Island on the Antarctic Peninsula.

These animals have overgrazed much of the grassland around the coast, thus destroying important breeding sites of the burrowing petrels and prions that feed offshore.

In contrast to the abandoned whaling stations, modern scientific bases are far from deserted. Indeed, man's invasion of the Antarctic is increasing every year. Nowadays, however, the emphasis is on science rather than exploitation. But there is still a threat to the wildlife. Bases ideally need to be built on a solid, ice-free promontory – just the kind of area on which penguins form their rookeries. At least one Antarctic base has already been built in the middle of a penguin colony, which creates disturbance and reduces the breeding potential of the penguin population.

Pollution is also a major problem as more nations jostle for space in comparatively accessible areas like the South Shetland Islands. Domestic waste, sewage and oil-spills all pollute the environment in the vicinity of many bases, while generators and diesel engines pump out toxic fumes into the once clean and pure Antarctic air.

Glossary

ADAPTATIONS Physical changes to an animal.

BLUBBER The layer of fat under an animal's skin.

BENTHIC Living on the seabed.

CRECHE A group of young chicks.

DILATE To increase the size of, for example, a blood vessel.

DOWN The soft, fluffy feathering on chicks.

ENVIRONMENT The surroundings of animals and plants.

FAST ICE An unbroken layer of frozen sea ice.

FLEDGE Of a chick, to grow adult feathers before leaving the nest.

FLOE A flat piece of floating ice.

HAREM A group of female seals.

ICECAP A large, stable body of ice on a solid rock base.

INCUBATE To sit on eggs to keep them warm and hatch them.

INSULATION Material that prevents the loss of heat.

PACK ICE Fast ice that has broken to form floes.

PHYTOPLANKTON Microscopic plants that live in water.

PREDATOR An animal that kills and eats other animals.

PUP A young seal.

REGURGITATE To bring up food from the stomach to the mouth.

SUCKLE To drink the mother's milk.

TERRITORY Piece of land which an animal defends against intruders.

WEAN To end the dependence of a young animal on its mother's milk.